JUBILEE

Fifty years of a classic London bus

By

JOHN REED

Produced in association with

LONDON TRANSPORT MUSEUM

Silver Link Publishing Ltd

**The Coach House,
Garstang Road, St Michael's,
Lancashire, PR3 OTG.**

Above: Piccadilly Circus, the hub of the Empire, in 1949. There are more buses than private cars in view in a year when LT buses carried 3,928 millon passengers. Shepherd's Bush garage's RTL232 nudges past a roof box RT to the east of the Circus while another RT can be seen in the distance in Regent Street. The other nine buses in view are an interesting pre-war mixture. The oldest, the six-wheel AEC Renown LT-type crossing the Circus, would have been in its last weeks of service as all the double-deck LTs had been replaced by January 1950. When one thinks of all the grandiose schemes put forward for Piccadilly Circus in the past 40 years the general scene, apart from the names on a few buildings, has changed very little. *LT Museum 662.*

Left: It is always good to finish work at the end of a long day, and after an evening taking Londoners home, many buses could stop work too. Peckham Garage is the scene here, early in 1953. After a hard day's work, some of Peckham's 120 buses enter the servicing lanes driven by night shift shunters. Lubricating oil is being fed to the engine through pressure guns. Diesel fuel is going into the tanks - refuelling took four minutes. Then, it was off for a wash, an internal clean and then over to the parking area to wait for the start of the next day. *LT Museum U54340.*

FRONT COVER: Henry Poole's figure of the Black Friar, perched on his ledge outside the pub of the same name, has been passed by RTs 3719 (right) and 2791 on route 168A, on April 4 1974. *R.C.Riley.*

TITLE PAGE (UPPER): The RT evolved through many design changes to reach its classic form, as illustrated in this mid-1950s view. *LT Museum H2867.* (LOWER): Green-liveried RT 3199 awaits departure from Beaconsfield, for Staines. *LT Museum 23263.*

AUTHOR'S ACKNOWLEDGEMENTS

I WAS particularly pleased to be invited to compile this celebration of the RT family of London buses in their Golden Jubilee year. Back in the 1950s, such a project would have been considered laughable, unthinkable even. How, for example, could 7,000 buses, which all looked very similar, merit a book of their own? Well, times and attitudes change and here we are in 1989, ready to remember fondly the days when standardisation was the watch-word on the buses, and there was no room inside for nonconformity. Who would have thought in those days that 30 years later we would have not only many different bus types running around in London, but also diverse liveries – and operators, too! But people *do* look back to the past with nostalgia and this book won't help anyone overcome a secret desire to return to London bus days gone by.

Now, on to the credits. Much of the photographic material used in this album has come from the London Transport Museum, whose archives I have plundered heavily. The LT collection spans more than a century-and-a-half of London's transport history (including the Underground) so the material featuring RTs represents only a minute proportion of the available material. A few shots may have been seen before; I'm not the first, nor will I be the last, to leave my 'dabs' on the Museum's micro-fiche, but I've done my best to eke out some previously unpublished photographs. My thanks to Sheila Taylor and Paul Castle at the Museum, for their help and patience.

I have also used some material from other photographers, notably: Alan B. Cross, Bruce Jenkins, Geoff Rixon, Lyndon Rowe and R.C. Riley, whose colour shot of London Bridge in 1955 (see page 8) can only be described as a' little gem.' My thanks to them as well, for their work has helped me produce a book which I hope will stand as a photographic reminder of, and a fond tribute to, the most prolific London buses ever built.

John Reed,
Southend-on-Sea, Essex, May 1989.

CONTENTS

Introduction......4
The RT on the Streets......14
'The Eight Footers'......19
Global Adventures......20
Buses for Trams......22
Heyday......25
At Home......29
Maintenance......34
Country Garages......37
Aldenham Works......40
Bus Stations......46
To the Airport......48
Fares Please......50
Inclement Weather......51
Question of Congestion......53
The 1958 Strike......55
Two Decades of Decline......56
Farewell......61
Revival in the '80s......62

© *Copyright John Reed/Silver Link Publishing Ltd.*

Designed by Peter Smith. Jacket Design by Nigel Harris.

First published in the United Kingdom, August 1989.

All rights reserved. No part of this publication may be reproduced, stored in a retrieval system, transmitted in any form, by any means electronic or mechanical, or photocopied, or recorded by any other information storage and retrieval system without prior permission in writing from the publisher.

Imagesetting by Ps&Qs, Liverpool, Merseyside, and printed in the United Kingdom by The Amadeus Press, Huddersfield, Yorkshire.

British Library Cataloguing in Publication Data
Reed, John, 1946-
RT Jubilee,
1. London. RT class buses, history
I. Title
629.2'2233'09421

ISBN 0 947971 38 6

INTRODUCTION

Above: On a murky April day in 1939, newly-completed RT1 was taken into Battersea Park and photographed. It was in its second livery, red with off-white central band and upper deck window pillars - the first had been a basic all red with silver horizontal beading stripes. The gentle contours and subtle curves must have been a real eyecatcher to the first onlookers. Interestingly, the bus carries a route number stencil, under the canopy. These appeared on the first production RTs but did not become a common feature until 1948. The route 164A blinds were only provided to make the bus look 'finished.' RT1 never worked on the 164A route, which in fact did not officially receive RTs until 1953! *LT Museum U29398 .*

Every new year brings the prospect of anniversaries to celebrate or at least mark in some way. In 1989 there were plenty to go round, some important and some seemingly trivial. Which description best fits the anniversary of a London bus is a matter of personal opinion. The bus in question, the RT, celebrates two anniversaries in 1989; it is 50 years since the first example entered passenger service, and it's ten years since they last did a day's work for London Transport.

Despite frequent moans and groans about services, Londoners have a 'soft spot' for their buses, even so, how many people would bring to mind the RT just by hearing those two magic letters? But show them a photograph and most would instantly recognise the RT as the bus which took them to school, shops, office or factory — and out in the evenings or at weekends to enjoy themselves. The RT was an important and indispensable part of everyday life in London for nearly 40 years.

The RT wasn't marketed or given an identity like the *Routemaster* which came after it. People weren't asked what they liked or disliked about it; the RT was simply *imposed* on London. But it was a very happy imposition for it was stamped with

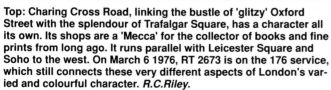

Top: Charing Cross Road, linking the bustle of 'glitzy' Oxford Street with the splendour of Trafalgar Square, has a character all its own. Its shops are a 'Mecca' for the collector of books and fine prints from long ago. It runs parallel with Leicester Square and Soho to the west. On March 6 1976, RT 2673 is on the 176 service, which still connects these very different aspects of London's varied and colourful character. *R.C.Riley.*

Above, left Newly-overhauled RTs always had a distinctive interior aroma, which lasted for a few weeks after they received 'the Aldenham treatment.' Was it the paint? The woodstain? The new

seat moquette or Rexine? - or a combination of them all? Whatever it was, it is no doubt wafting through the saloons of RT 4063, seen in ex-works condition at Kilburn in May 1967. *Geoff Rixon.*

Above, right: A fair number of the 484 RTs which London Country inherited from LT in 1970 were repainted, some were even overhauled. The cream centre band was replaced by one of yellow and the new LC symbol was applied to the offside rear panel. RT 4515 is seen passing through Hatfield, displaying the new style, on September 6 1971. *R. C. Riley.*

the hallmark of good design and reliability, and although the passing of London Transport's last RT in 1979 wasn't marked with the same outburst of widespread affection as were the farewells of London's trams and trolleybuses, the RT has firmly established itself in London's transport history. It was the first, and the last, mass-produced standard London bus. At its zenith, the RT family totalled more than 7,000 vehicles – 4,000 more than the final score of *Routemasters*.

The RT was a continuation of the steady design process which began in the early 1900s. Until the 1930s, London bus development was spearheaded by the London General Omnibus Company, then London's largest bus undertaking. Development was both remarkable and rapid. With its subsidiary company (the chassis and engine builder AEC) the 'General' developed and built no fewer than eight major double-deck bus types in the 24 years from 1909 until its absorption into the London Passenger Transport Board in 1933. By then the 28hp petrol-engined chassis of the 1910 B-type had evolved into the 108bhp diesel-engined STL of 1932.

The creation of the LPTB, which soon became known as London Transport, brought together a *pot pourri* of buses consisting of the well established 'General' types, plus many others inherited from smaller, independent companies. By the mid-1930s, it was apparent that some kind of standardisation was needed to make maintenance of an ever-growing bus fleet both easier and quicker.

To this end, AEC and London Transport developed a new double-deck chassis with an 8.8 litre diesel engine and with gear change and braking controlled by compressed air. The new chassis, named Regent Mark III (the abbreviation 'Regent Three' giving rise to the term 'RT') boasted many other new features too, like automatic lubrication. All were put to the test when the chassis, married to a 56-seat open staircase body, entered service on route 18B (Wembley, Empire Pool - Hanwell Garage) in July 1938.

Some modifications were later made to the chassis, including the

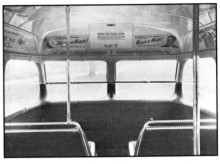

Above: Inside, both upstairs and down, RT1 was quite a revelation. The curves and contours were perpetuated on everything in sight. The aim was to make cleaning easier and eliminate dirt traps. The colour scheme of brown rexine side panels, green and cream rexine on the window pillars and cream ceilings, finished off with a thin red band all around was eventually applied to the entire RT family. The seat moquette changed pattern with the production buses and became the style long associated with the RTs. The best bargain has to be the Green Line Coach Guide at 2d (1p). Most people could afford to smoke, 15 Minors cost 6d (2.5p), but you had to be rich to spit! *LT Museum Nos. 15123/18147.*

fitting of a more powerful 9.6 litre engine, and by April 1939 it was ready to receive a new body, a handsome 55-seater of a revolutionary new design, reflecting classic 1930s streamlining. The only square corners were found on the front and rear roof number boxes and on the AEC/LT triangular badge on the grille. Whereas many previous London bus designs, stylish as they were, looked like a collection of bits bolted together, the new bus, numbered RT1, looked both complete and satisfying to the eye. RT1 spent the summer of 1939 being 'put through its paces,' then on August 9 1939 it entered service from Putney Chelverton Road Garage on Route 22 (Putney-Homerton).

By the end of 1939, LT's Chiswick Works was busy building 'production' RTs. There were only minor design differences to RT1, but by the time the production models began entering service from Chelverton Road and Putney Bridge Garages early in 1940, more important matters dominated the world's attention. The war had begun on September 3 that year, and bus building, along with many other activities not immediately relevant to the war effort, slowed or ceased altogether. Only 150 of the original order for 350 RTs were built by the time production was halted in 1942. But huge sums of money had been spent developing the RT and the project did not die, but was merely suspended 'for the duration.'

In 1944, with the war turning in favour of the Allies, London Transport

Above: A rear view of an early production RT, one of 150 examples built between 1939 and 1942, which eventually became known as the pre-war RTs. This is RT33 outside Victoria Garage on January 7 1943, complete with blackout markings. Its rear roof route number box is still being properly used, but within a short while nearly all London's buses were fitted with just one blind in each display area and the unused apertures painted over. It wasn't until 1950 that full blind displays appeared again. Just visible under the used ticket box is a notice confirming that between 8 and 12 people could stand inside at permitted times. The war had brought about an overall reduction in bus services and thereby a relaxation of the usual 'five only' standing restrictions. *LT Museum U34437.*

Above: The 1948 batch of RTs had a revised canopy, incorporating a route number box above the front lower saloon window. The canopy fairing was removed to make the box more visible. Gleaming new RT989, in green country livery, is at Chiswick works on October 14 1948. It was already fitted with blinds for Northfleet garage from where it entered service later that month. *LT Museum U45018.*

ordered 1,000 Regent III chassis from AEC for delivery as soon as conditions permitted. The first arrived in March 1946 but delivery was slow. Chiswick was no longer building new bus bodies, and was concentrating instead on the mammoth task of rebuilding and overhauling existing buses ailing from an overdose of wartime neglect. The job of constructing the bodies for the next generation of RTs was given to two outside manufacturers, the west London company Park Royal Vehicles and Weymanns of Addlestone, Surrey. Both companies were given identical specifications. It took some months for the two concerns to plan, organise and begin production and it was not until April 28 1947 that the first complete post-war RT arrived from the Weymann factory.

The new bus differed in several ways from the prewar model, but the pedigree was still visible. From May,

when the first new RTs entered service on route 10 (Victoria Station-Abridge), until November 1954, when the last examples left Weymanns factory, a steady stream of new buses arrived for service with LT. In fact, the final total of post-war bodies built was 6820, and although in number the RT family was to constitute the largest standardised bus fleet anywhere in the world at the time, the urgency with which LT needed new buses did bring about some diversity. Three other manufacturers, Cravens of York, Metro Cammell of Birmingham and Saunders Engineering of Anglesey, were contracted to build RT bodies. Of these, only the 120 built by Cravens, with their 'top-heavy' look and extra side windows, were immediately distinguishable from the others.

AECs position as the traditional London bus chassis supplier had been

challenged when the London Passenger Transport Board was established in 1933, for the new undertaking was obliged to buy a proportion of its bus chassis from other companies. Leyland Motors, one of Britain's biggest bus manufacturers, naturally benefited from this, and LT had duly purchased both single and double-deck bus chassis from Leyland since the 1930s.

Early in 1947, London Transport placed an order with Leyland for 1,500 chassis based on the company's tried and tested PD2 unit. So it was that on June 16 1948 the RT ceased to be a 'class' and became a 'family' – for on that day a new bus entered service from Turnham Green Garage bearing a familiar RT body but running on a Leyland PD2/1 chassis. The bus was given the number RTL 501 and its only visible difference to the original RT was the new shape

INTRODUCTION

On a sunny day in May 1955, Dick Riley was standing on London Bridge photographing ships in the Thames when sudden inspiration prompted him to turn and press the shutter on the bustle behind him. So, frozen in time, in colour, is a scene with at least eight RT family buses, possibly in a traffic jam, but typifying the Golden Age of standardisation on London's buses. *R.C.Riley.*

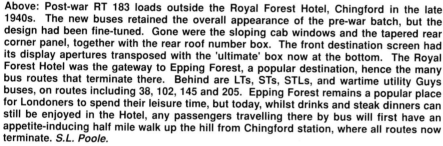

Above: Post-war RT 183 loads outside the Royal Forest Hotel, Chingford in the late 1940s. The new buses retained the overall appearance of the pre-war batch, but the design had been fine-tuned. Gone were the sloping cab windows and the tapered rear corner panel, together with the rear roof number box. The front destination screen had its display apertures transposed with the 'ultimate' box now at the bottom. The Royal Forest Hotel was the gateway to Epping Forest, a popular destination, hence the many bus routes that terminate there. Behind are LTs, STs, STLs, and wartime utility Guys buses, on routes including 38, 102, 145 and 205. Epping Forest remains a popular place for Londoners to spend their leisure time, but today, whilst drinks and steak dinners can still be enjoyed in the Hotel, any passengers travelling there by bus will first have an appetite-inducing half mile walk up the hill from Chingford station, where all routes now terminate. *S.L. Poole.*

Above: Surprisingly, although a decision to modify the RT front destination screen to incorporate all the information in one sectioned panel was taken late in 1946, the first buses to sport the new style did not leave the Park Royal factory until October 1948. The new destination layout was the last major design change in the standard RT, illustrated by this view of Weymann-bodied RT 2138, by the pond at Hampstead Heath early in 1949. *LT Museum 17316.*

Leyland grille at the front. RTL 501 was the first of an eventual 1,630 7ft 6in wide Leyland chassis' supplied to LT between 1948 and 1954. The bodies fitted to these chassis were from the usual suppliers, either Park Royal or Weymann, with the addition of Metro Cammell, who also built 500 bodies to the basic RT pattern in 1949/50.

The 1947 Leyland order included 500 eight feet wide chassis, a further development of the PD2. Despite a Metropolitan Police restriction on the operation of eight feet wide buses in busy areas, London Transport realised that wider buses had specific advantages, and pressed ahead, After all, the police had objected in the past to innovations like covered top decks and enclosed drivers cabs, but they had later changed their views on these, so why not again? Leyland was also contracted to build the bodies for the 'eight footers' and on May 11 1949 the first of the new buses entered service on route 41 (Hornsey Rise-Ilford Station).

It had been intended to give the 8ft Leylands the sequence RTL 1-500, and incorporate the narrower buses in the same class from thereon (hence the numbering of RTL 501, already mentioned) but in the event they were given their own classification as RTW ('W' for wide). The body styling of the RTWs was similar to other members of the RT family, both inside and out.

By 1949, RT bodies were being supplied at a faster rate than the chassis, so it was decided to mount new bodies on redundant STL chassis and create a new 'SRT' class. The result was exactly what one might expect from a small capacity engine trying to power a body heavier than the one it was designed to carry; an attractive but sluggish vehicle which bus crews came to view with disdain. Although the 160 SRTs eventually built survived for several years, they were kept away from the more hilly routes and used only sparingly outside the 'rush hours.'

The RT family was thus complete,

and as the 1950s proceeded RTs in red, green or Green Line colours could be seen everywhere in London Transport's sprawling 1980 square mile area. By mid-1955, RTs had replaced every pre-war and wartime double-decker in LT's massive fleet. They had also displaced the capital's trams and by this stage the oldest RTs themselves were starting to disappear, for all the pre-war RTs were withdrawn from service by May 1955, many joining the LT driver training fleet.

In the autumn of 1955 the maximum number of RT family buses ever in service at any one time - 6,180 - was scheduled. It was the mid-century bus, but it was also susceptible to mid-century bus problems including, worst of all, a drop in passenger numbers, staff shortages and traffic delays. From the second half of the 1950s the story becomes one of decline and disposal, albeit very gradual.

Sadly there never was a time when all the RTs built were in service

Above: Pausing at traffic lights in Charing Cross Road at St Giles Circus is SRT 147, a mix of two very different animals. The SRT class can best be described as a well-intentioned mistake. They were sadly under-powered and not popular with crews. All 160 had gone by August 1954, but the standard RT bodies were given a new lease of life on new chassis in the last days of RT production. Evocative of the era are the adverts for Peek Frean's 'famous biscuits.' *Alan B. Cross.*

Above, left: The Craven RTs were very different in appearance to the vehicles produced elsewhere. They had a squarer, more clumsy appearance, and because their body design was non-standard they were prime candidates for withdrawal when a passenger numbers declined in the mid-1950s. Green RT 1406, based at Watford High Street garage, was specially posed in June 1950 in one of the anonymous locations so favoured by LTs official photographers. By then, all the 120 Craven RTs had been delivered. *LT Museum 1414.*

Above, right: New Saunders-bodied RT 1155 stands in Croydon Garage on March 4 1949. Saunders RTs, 300 of which were delivered to LT between 1948 and 1951, were easily distinguishable (on the offside at least) by the position of the route number stencil which was placed further back from the side windows than on other RTs. Also, Saunders RT body panels and beading had diagonally placed screw fixing holes (a point for the enthusiast, perhaps!) just visible in the picture. This unusual feature meant that special stocks of body panels had to be kept to replace any damaged in accidents. *LT Museum 46359.*

Left: There were 2,131 Leyland members of the RT family. Most common were the RTLs, with their standard RT bodies. Hammersmith (Riverside) garage, along with Sidcup and West Green (all sadly no longer in existence) were amongst the first to operate the Leyland-built vehicles. Riverside's RTL74 was photographed on January 27 1949 at work on route 17. The utility blind, a legacy from wartime economies, gives little away about the geography of the route. *LT Museum H16274.*

together. The last examples off the production lines in 1954 were sent straight into store, for there was nothing for them to do. The number of people using buses was decreasing at this time as Britons, basking in more prosperity and leisure, bought an ever increasing range of domestic and leisure goods including cars and television sets, two items which effectively ended the need for many people to travel by bus to work or away from their homes for entertainment. A seven-week bus strike over pay and conditions in May and June 1958 only accelerated the process. When the strike ended, LT withdrew 20 routes and put a huge selection of redundant RTs and RTLs up for sale.

The following year, when LT began replacing trolleybuses, it was vehicles from the RT family (not the next generation bus specially designed for the purpose, the *Routemaster*) which were used to convert the first routes. Full scale *Routemaster* production started in 1959, the year the last 'new' RTs, which had been in store for some five years, entered service. Routemasters replaced the remaining trolleybuses and eventually most of

the RTLs and RTWs. In February 1968 when the last *Routemaster* was delivered there were still around 3,700 RTs and RTLs which included the vast country region stretching from Slough and Windsor in the west right across to Gravesend and Grays in the east, and from Hitchin right down to Horsham.

From January 1 1970, the country area became part of the National Bus Company and 484 RTs were transferred to its new subsidiary company, London Country Bus Services Ltd. By 1970, both LT and LCBS were busy converting as many bus routes as possible to driver-only operation, initially using large capacity single-deck buses, and RT replacement gathered speed. But it was to take a further nine years for the RT to be completely ousted, if not by driver-only buses then by *Routemasters* made redundant by their introduction elsewhere. There were several stays of execution but the end finally came on April 7 1979, and it was fitting that the very last RTs, running on route 62 (Barking-Barkingside), were replaced by *Routemasters*. The logical progression had reached its conclusion – or

at least so everyone thought.

For in 1989 you can still enjoy a ride on an RT, as by a strange paradox which makes transport affairs so interesting and unpredictable, Government bus route tendering procedure has given new companies with new ideas and aims the opportunity to run scheduled bus services. Thus, Two Essex-based companies, Ensignbus of Purfleet and Blue Triangle of Rainham, run RTs on suitable occasions, the latter on a regular basis on summer Sundays on contract services for Essex County Council.

Also many RTs, RTLs and even a few RTWs are in the capable hands of preservationists ensuring for posterity that there is at least one example of every type made still in existence to examine enjoy - and, if you are lucky, travel on!

Half a century on and the RT story is anything but a closed book; nor is it ever likely to be while there is still such a wealth of admiration and enthusiasm surrounding what is, after all, the finest family of double deck buses ever built.

INTRODUCTION

Right: Metro-Cammell built 450 bodies for the RTL class. They were easily distinguished by their thinner centre band. In most other respects the 'Met Camm' bodies were identical to those built by Park Royal/Weymann, but because of their construction they could not be exchanged on overhaul with those from other manufacturers. They were thus always confined to their own modified chassis within the RTL class. By the time RTL 993 was delivered in January 1951, new buses were clad in less stylish all-over red or green liveries, broken only by the centre cream band. The bus is departing from the former tram stopping bay at Turnpike Lane on September 26 1951, with a standard Park Royal-bodied Leyland still in its original colours behind. *Alan B. Cross.*

Above: One pleasant feature boasted by the Green Line RTs was the detachable bullseye motif fitted to the centre side panels. Later RT additions to the Green Line fleet were painted in the same colours but received only a transfer bullseye. *LT Museum 247/2.*

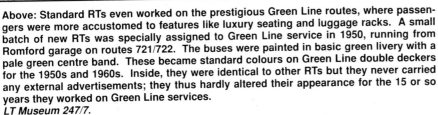

Above: Standard RTs even worked on the prestigious Green Line routes, where passengers were more accustomed to features like luxury seating and luggage racks. A small batch of new RTs was specially assigned to Green Line service in 1950, running from Romford garage on routes 721/722. The buses were painted in basic green livery with a pale green centre band. These became standard colours on Green Line double deckers for the 1950s and 1960s. Inside, they were identical to other RTs but they never carried any external advertisements; they thus hardly altered their appearance for the 15 or so years they worked on Green Line services. *LT Museum 247/7.*

Right: The extra six inches of the eight feet wide RTWs gave the class a distinctly chunky appearance, and yet it is difficult to tell at a glance where the extra six inches are, so closely did Leyland conceal them in following the overall RT design concept. RTW1 was photographed when new in April 1949. *LT Museum 16543.*

Above: As the years passed the RT family succumbed to a number of retrograde changes in appearance. First to disappear was the cream upper deck window surrounds, followed some years later by another pleasant feature, the polished chrome/aluminium wheel hub rings. This 1962 profile of RT 1915, shows the livery retained by the RT family for the remainder of its LT service. The only major change to follow came in 1964 when the cream band gave way to one of pale grey. *LT Museum 13970.*

Above and right: Blind displays also changed, along with the livery. A full display utilising every available aperture was reintroduced in 1950, and initially the front display for many routes included a five line upper case via point blind. This was reduced to four lines in 1957/58, with upper/lower case lettering becoming the norm from 1961, although some RTs could still be seen with upper case via blinds right up until the early 1970s. These two photographs illustrate the transition. *LT Museum U44946/X591.*

THE RT ON THE STREETS

Below: With only 151 examples in service before 1947, the RTs were easily lost amongst LT's 8,000 other red buses and trolley-buses of the day. Here at King's Cross in July 1947, two pre-war RTs are in view. One, partially obscured by an STL on route 68, is still in its original livery, a variation on that applied to RT1, which includes off-white lower deck window surrounds and a brown roof (a wartime addition). The RT nearest the camera has been repainted in the post-war red livery. Also visible are a 20-seat CR single decker, possibly working as an extra on route 73, and a B2 class short-wheelbase trolleybus of a type specially designed for work on hilly routes, like the 615 up to Parliament Hill Fields. *LT Museum 17994.*

Right: The first green-liveried RTs entered service in LT's country area during July 1948. Hemel Hempstead garage, in Hertfordshire, represented here by RT 616 in Watford, being one of the first recipients. Behind the RT is a *Bluebird* ST, one of 23 similar buses built for London General's Country Services in 1932, and both are pausing outside a rather fine household store which among other things was a drysalter, a dealer in dyes, oils, pickles, gums and tinned meats. You won't find J. Salmon, nor any of his relatives, selling dyes to the people of Watford in 1989. Today, the site is occupied by a fast food restaurant selling hamburgers, a delicacy virtually unknown on this side of the Atlantic back in 1948. *C.F. Clapper Collection.*

Left: As early as 1935, London Transport was making known its intention to rid London of its trams in favour of trolleybuses within ten years. But things did not go quite as planned, and there were still plenty of trams grinding around in the early 1950s. So, for a time, RT and tramcar co-existed. On July 22 1949, Nunhead garage-based RT 2182 meets with two trams at Elephant and Castle, once renowned as one of the busiest tramway junctions in south London. To the right, outside the tube station, is an original London County Council tram stop, still in place a full 16 years after the Council ceased to be responsible for operating London's trams.
Alan B. Cross.

Above: If you're composing a picture, you can't go wrong if you include lots of children! Perhaps that's why this one was taken, to show London Transport as a caring organisation which looked after its younger passengers. Everyone seems to be enjoying themselves, except the little boy about to get on. He's probably a little shy, amongst all the girls. RT 1121 is displaying posters for National Savings, as carried by many buses in the late 1940s and early 1950s, the Government being anxious that everyone should try to rebuild their post-war lives on solid financial foundations. This contrived but happy scene was photographed in 1949, probably in Southgate.
LT Museum U47569.

THE RT ON THE STREETS

Below: Apart from the vehicles, this view from Victoria Street looking towards Parliament Square has hardly altered in the 40 years since the photograph was taken. RT 222 is making for Pimlico on May 9 1950, displaying advertisements for the picture news magazine *Everybody's*. Just a glance at similar pictures of buses taken around this period will reveal the names of similar journals like *John Bull, Picture Post* and *Illustrated*. With the advent of TV, and instant visual news, the need for news magazines declined and most had gone by the early 1960s. *LT Museum 1332.*

Right: This is Oxford Circus in 1951, with standardisation taking hold. RTs and RTWs predominate, whilst the odd man out is the 1930s STL on route 6. More modern taxi-cabs are also in view and make an interesting contrast with the pre-war leather-top cabs with their miniscule back windows. In 1989, Buses and taxis can still go in both directions along Oxford Street and turn right into Regent Street from the west. But if you are in a private car, and want to keep within the law, you must take a more circuitous route to get from one end of Oxford Street to the other. *LT Museum 2807.*

Left: Tower Bridge, based on an original design by the architect Sir Horace Jones, is the gateway to the pool of London and a 'must' for any visitor to the capital. It is still traversed by route 78 but you won't find RT1660 anywhere in sight today. RTs last worked on the 78 service in 1972, 20 years after this view was photographed. *LT Museum H16345.*

Below: Brand new RT 3204 shows off the new all-over green livery at Uxbridge station on July 1 1950. What a pity colour photography was not as widely available as it is today! *Alan B. Cross.*

Right: When the last tram ran through the Kingsway tram subway on April 6 1952, the unique tunnel, which ran under the Aldwych and connected the Embankment with Southampton Row, was closed. The replacement buses on routes 171 and 172 were routed by Temple station and round the Aldwych at street level. The Embankment entrance to the subway is just out of view under Waterloo Bridge in this June 1952 view. In 1989, you can still stand at the Southampton Row end of the subway and look down into the old tunnel, complete with its rusting tram tracks, as a memorial to times past. *LT Museum 15011.*

THE RT ON THE STREETS

Below: Don't bother to count them! There are more than 55 double-deckers in this view of Trafalgar Square on June 6 1953, Coronation Day for HM Queen Elizabeth II. Close scrutiny with a magnifying glass reveals that only three are not members of the RT family. It was a remarkable achievement on the part of London Transport and the bus manufacturers that in just six years since the first post-war RT was delivered, 5,120 out of the central area fleet of 5,734 scheduled buses on Monday to Friday belonged to the RT family. Already post war 'dream' cars like Ford *Consuls* and Austin *Devons* are beginning to 'clog the arteries' and prevent free movement of the buses, albeit in rather unusual circumstances. The traffic problems which were later to cast a shadow over London's buses were not quite above the horizon in 1953. *LT Museum 13912.*

Right: Fleet Street, the world of hacks, hot metal, deadlines, spiked stories and *El Vino's*, looks strangely tranquil for ten to five in the afternoon. What a pity that the actual date is not recorded; all we know is that the shot was taken in June 1952. If we knew the date we'd know what the day's 'hot' news story was. One big story in June '52 was the first publication of the harrowing wartime Diaries of Anne Frank. There was also a host of minor newsworthy developments, some of which are still part of life today, like the introduction of blinking beacons at zebra crossings. And, of course, cricket; Denis Compton hit his hundredth century on June 11 that year. Today, Fleet Street is almost dead, as far as the production of papers is concerned. All the big 'nationals' have moved, either eastwards to Docklands or west to Kensington. Many of the giant offices lie empty and silent, including the black glass edifice of the *Daily Express* and the most impressive one of all, *The Daily Telegraph* building. The RT on route 13 has just passed the office of an early Fleet Street casualty, the *News Chronicle* and *Star*, the latter at the time being London's third evening paper behind the *Evening Standard* and *Evening News*. Some readers will remember the cry: "Star, News, Standard!"? Both the *Star*, and its daily companion the *News Chronicle*, closed in 1960. *LT Museum 15417.*

'THE EIGHT FOOTERS'

WHEN the eight feet wide RTWs were first delivered, they were allocated to suburban garages including Barking, Bromley, Seven Kings and Southall, and used on routes which kept them out of congested areas. The police needed to be satisfied that the extra six inches did not pose any road safety problems in busy narrow streets. In 1950, London Transport conducted three separate trials on selected routes in central London and the City to prove that the RTWs did not threaten road safety. The trials were a resounding success and the RTWs were later moved over to busy trunk routes like the 6, 8, 14 and 22, routes where their more spacious interiors soon found favour with the customers.

Above: For a time after the 1950 'width' trials, the RTWs continued to run on suburban services. The extra inches pose no problem as RTW 437, in all red livery, purrs along a deserted suburban avenue in Harrow during October that year. *LT Museum H16608.*

Above: By 1952, RTWs had taken up their rightful place on some of central London's busiest routes. All seems fairly tranquil here though as an 'eight footer' working on route 74 passes the Victoria and Albert Museum, in Kensington, on its way to Camden Town in August 1952. *LT Museum 24573.*

Above: In June/July 1950, the RTW trials were carried out, on routes passing through Shaftesbury Avenue, and included the 14, 19, 22 and 38 services. Here, RTW156 crosses the path of two pre-war taxicabs and a 1949 six cylinder Vauxhall Velox, on its way into Piccadilly. The advert gives food for thought to those who believe the word 'Fab' was an invention of the Beatles or Cathy McGowan! *LT Museum U49519.*

GLOBAL ADVENTURES

Above: Making cautious progress across a cobbled square 'somewhere in northern Europe' during the first overseas trip by London buses in 1950, is RT 1702. The bus is about to pass a German-built Volkswagen saloon, a car with much in common to the RT, including an absence of square edges and corners in its rounded design. Like the RT, the VW was conceived during the mid-1930s, its prototype appeared in 1938 and it too had a limited pre-war production run before the factory which built it was turned over to producing military vehicles. After the war, thanks largely to the British occupying forces in Germany, the Volkswagen project was resumed and by 1950 *Beetles* were being sold throughout the world, a true 'peoples car'. To date more than 20 million Beetles have been made, of which half or more are apparently still in existence. Perhaps the one in the photograph is still around - RT 1702 certainly is; it is privately preserved!
LT Museum 14241.

THE Second World War tore Europe apart and many of the ties which had existed in the long ago pre-war days took time and considerable diplomatic effort to heal. The early 1950s were, perhaps, looked upon as the dawn of a new age, an opportunity to rebuild the damage left by the war – and not just in material terms. The Festival of Britain in 1951 provided a not-to-be-missed chance to show Europe and the world that Britain was still very much in business and at the forefront of new technology and industry. The country was also a pleasant place to visit and what more novel example of a 'new' Britain could you transport overseas to act as an ambassador than a shiny new red London bus?

So, the early 1950s were marked by a series of overseas visits to promote Britain and British wares, sponsored by British firms. The first tour, to publicise the Festival of Britain, began in July 1950 and involved four brand new RTs on an eight-country, 4,000 mile tour of Northern Europe, including Scandinavia, Holland, Belgium, Luxembourg, Denmark, France and West Germany. Later in 1950 a couple of RTWs made a trip to the Berlin Trade Fair. This was followed in 1952 by probably the most famous of all the overseas trips, a three bus (two RTs and one RTL) tour of the USA and Canada, primarily to attract visitors to Britain. Trade Fairs in Switzerland and Sweden were visited by an RT and an RTL during the summer of 1953. RT 4760 attended the Maastricht Fair in Holland in June 1954 and the following year RTL 1117 made a three month tour of Holland.

1957 was the last year any organised tours involving the RT family took place. RT 2422 made a one month trip to a Trade Fair in northern Holland in June and July. It was only back in London for a month before it was off again, in the company of RTL1486, this time to Finland for a British Trade Fair in Helsinki. The buses arrived back in the UK on October 4 1957, after giving countless rides to eager Finns, many of whom had probably never seen a double deck bus before, or have since. With their arrival, RT family sojourns away from these shores, at least in London Transport ownership, were at an end and the honour passed to LT's new pride, the *Routemaster.*

Above: RTW 421 is causing a few heads to turn as it proceeds along a Berlin strasse during its visit to the Berlin Trade Fair in the autumn of 1950. Although the war had been over for five years, there are still a few signs of the Allied bombing raids of the darker age, a few holes in the tops of buildings, half missing church spires and so on. The Berlin visit was the only occasion the handsome RTWs left Britain whilst in LT ownership. There were obviously no qualms about the suitability of their eight foot girth in the wide thoroughfares of Berlin. *LT Museum 16686.*

Right: It could be the outskirts of a sleepy Cotswold village, but it is many thousands of miles away from Stow-on-the-Wold! This is the Henry Ford village at Greenfield, Detroit, in the USA. RT 2776 was one of three buses which made the 12,000 mile trip across the Atlantic to New York and thence to Washington, Cincinatti, St. Louis, Kansas, Santa Fe, Grand Canyon to Hollywood. The bus then travelled to San Francisco and back via Salt Lake City, Denver, Omaha, Milwakee, Chicago, Detroit, Toledo, Syracuse, Boston and back to New York taking in some Canadian cities on the way. RT 2776 had completed most of the strenuous trip by the time it reached Greenfield. In true fashion the Americans had fitted it with air conditioning louvres as it was the one bus out of the three chosen to give the rides. RT 2776, complete with its unique ventilation, retained its original body until January 1969 when 'eyebrows' (as the body was christened) was fitted after overhaul to RT1708. No matter, the feature made it easily the most recognisable RT of them all. Sadly, no one bothered to preserve this very distinctive bus and it went for scrap in 1974. *LT Museum 24561.*

BUSES FOR TRAMS

IF IT HADN'T been for the war, London's trams would have all been replaced by 1943 and, just like north of the river, south London might well have been a mecca for the trolleybus. As it was, fate gave the trams a ten year reprieve for, after the war, LT decided initially to concentrate its efforts on replacing London's oldest double-deckers, the STs, LTs and some STLs, a process which was more or less completed early in 1950. After that, plans were drawn up for the replacement of the capital's remaining tram routes by diesel buses rather than new trolleybuses. At the beginning of 1950 there were still 740 trams

required for the busy weekday rush-hour services on more than 40 routes, the majority of which ran south of the river. The first part of an eight stage replacement programme took place on the night of September 30 1950. At each stage new RTs or RTLs replaced the trams and usually tram depots were converted to handle motor buses.

During the tram conversion programme two new garages were opened in south London and were used to provide buses for the new services. One was Thornton Heath, a former tram depot, which had closed in 1949 and was extensively rebuilt to

operate buses. It opened in time for Stage Three in April 1951. Stockwell, the other new garage, opened at Stage Seven in April 1953.

Two other garages featured in the tram replacement programme. Both were in Peckham. One was a former bus garage rebuilt as a result of wartime bombing. It reopened on May 2 1951. The other had been a former permanent way depot in Rye Lane. It was converted into a bus garage and opened for business at Stage Six on January 6 1952, when it provided most of the replacement buses for the new routes introduced from that date.

Above: Stage One of the tram replacement programme centred on Clapham and Wandsworth depots, which from the October 1 1950 became bus garages. At Clapham, new RTLs pose next to some of the trams they will replace just a few hours later. It would be interesting to know whether the onlookers approved of the new buses, for the end of London's trams was met with very mixed feelings. *LT Museum 1761.*

Right: At Wandsworth, more than 75 brand new RTs were drafted in to replace the trams. Here, RT 3269, is being moved sideways across the depot on the transverser used hitherto to move trams to and from the depot service bay. *LT Museum 24559.*

Left: In the early hours of October 1, the throbbing tones of the 9.6 litre AEC Regent III engine heralds the beginning of the end for London's trams, as RT 3272 edges out of Wandsworth garage to work one of the first journeys on new bus route 44. *LT Museum 1751.*

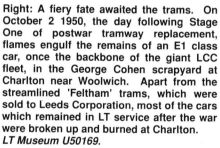

Right: A fiery fate awaited the trams. On October 2 1950, the day following Stage One of postwar tramway replacement, flames engulf the remains of an E1 class car, once the backbone of the giant LCC fleet, in the George Cohen scrapyard at Charlton near Woolwich. Apart from the streamlined 'Feltham' trams, which were sold to Leeds Corporation, most of the cars which remained in LT service after the war were broken up and burned at Charlton. *LT Museum U50169.*

Right: New RT 2553 departs from Peckham on what could have been the first journey on bus route 188, on July 11 1951, as some fairly important people (judging by their formal appearance) have gathered to see it off. *LT Museum U51877.*

Above, left: It took just 22 months to replace London's remaining trams. The last routes to go were based at Abbey Wood and New Cross depots. In the days leading up to the last day, Saturday July 5 1952, all the doomed trams were covered with posters, printed in red, proclaiming that this was their final week. Here ex-Leyton Corporation E3 class car number 169 grinds along the Embankment on New Cross depot's route 40 with an RTL at work in the background on the 168 service, a route introduced during the first stage of post-war tram replacement nearly two years before. *LT Museum 22787.*

Above, right: If those who travelled regularly on the New Cross and Abbey Wood trams were hoping for brand new buses as replacements, they were disappointed. Although some new buses were used, a number of older RTs, including some pre-war examples, and even some STLs, arrived to take over from the trams. These included pre-war RT 35, equipped with a full blind display but still clad in early post-war livery. It had stopped near New Cross garage on July 14 1952, just over a week after London's very last tram had made its final run. *Alan. B. Cross.*

HEYDAY

Below: Hyde Park Corner in 1954, and a typical London bus scene of the time. The scene includes aluminium tube Q-type shelters, contoured concrete bus stop posts with 'boat' shaped flags on top, complete with enamel route number plates slotted into the frame; and, of course, lots of RTs, including RT 1943, with dented roof dome, on its way to Mill Hill. It was rare to see any significant body damage on London's buses during this period. The routes serving the stop nearest the camera haven't changed much in 35 years. The 14, 30 and 74 still serve Hyde Park Corner today, as do the 9, 52 and 73 (almost!) featured on the other stop, but route 96 (Redbridge Station-Putney Common) was a casualty of the 1958 bus strike. The 297 was a night time service, renumbered N97 in September 1960. After this, LT used many of the high 200 series numbers, the night route renumbering scheme released for its new 'buses for trolleybuses' replacement routes. *LT Museum 15082.*

Left: Park Lane, leading to Marble Arch, carried two-way traffic in the 1950s, but today it is an impressive dual carriageway with the northbound lane separated from the southbound by an expanse of green. When RT 3924 was photographed in the Summer of 1954, full use was being made of the slipboard under the canopy by the front lower deck window. In their time RTs carried a variety of information on slipboards to advertise short term attractions and sports fixtures close to the routes they worked. The Oval has been a cricket venue since 1845, and at one time football was played there too. Probably the oddest function ever performed by the Oval ground was during World War II when it was used as a prisoner of war camp.
LT Museum H16827.

Below: Standardisation of the London bus is no longer a dream. RTs, RTLs and RTWs galore fill the scene as far as the eye can see. There are 16 buses on view in this quarter-mile stretch of Oxford Street, captured by LT's photographer in September 1954. The bus in the foreground, RT 3467, is a perfect example of the standard London bus of the mid-1950s. The ingredients: gleaming all-red livery, full blind display, polished wheel hubs and rims, leather grille covers for cold weather, canopy slipboard and fully utilised advertising panels. Although the character of the street hasn't altered, you can still buy anything from a thimble to a three piece suite; some of the shops have gone, among them Marshall & Snellgrove and Bourne & Hollingsworth. Countless smaller shops have come and gone too, but Selfridges and John Lewis trade on. *LT Museum 17827.*

Right: Obscuring the tasteful curves of Broadcasting House, in this 1954 view of Upper Regent Street, is RT 3787 working on route 159 from Streatham garage. The actual date is unrecorded, so we can only imagine some of the radio programmes which might have been on the Light Programme (the 1950s equivalent of Radio Two) at this time. The period is regarded by many as the golden age of radio comedy - it was the era of shows like *Ray's A Laugh, Take It From Here, Life With The Lyons,* and *A Life of Bliss.* More off-beat comedy was available too: Peter Ustinov and Peter Jones starred in (and wrote) *In All Directions,* and *The Goon Show* was keeping thousands of people at home on Tuesday nights. BBC executives may well have been discussing the prospects of a new radio comedy series planned for November 1954. *Hancock's Half Hour* was about to make Tony Hancock into a household name, and a comedy legend for many years to come. *LT Museum 16365.*

Left: There was a time when you could travel to many parts of London by bus on Christmas Day, and Saturday December 25 1954 was no exception. Sutton Garage's RT 4657 idles away a few seconds in deserted Morden on route 156, a circular service which started and finished at Morden Station. On Christmas Day 1954, most of the routes which ran, and quite a few did, began about 8.00 am, finishing by 4.00 pm - but not the 156. The last bus returned to Sutton garage at 10.29pm! It was one of only a handful of routes still running after 4.00 pm. Others included the 53, 76 and the outer suburban 150 which was still pounding between Ilford and Barkingside (The Old Maypole) until 10.25 pm on that cold and deserted Saturday night.
Alan B. Cross.

Above: Hyde Park Corner has always been a busy junction. Today, traffic flows around the arch on a huge gyratory system; there is also an underpass linking Piccadilly with Knightsbridge. In September 1956, when this view was taken, traffic flowed both ways past the arch. Two RTLs are heading for Grosvenor Place and Victoria in hot pursuit of an Austin *Cambridge* saloon. The route 52 bus has already been fitted with the new style four-line 'via' blind. Is it any easier to read than the 'five liner' still in use on the route 2 bus?
LT Museum 15083.

Left: The Embankment on July 4 1958, and with an eight week bus strike over (it ended on June 21) some Londoners were using their buses to the full once again. However, many preferred their own transport, and you can draw your own conclusions from the fact that only about seven of the cars on the move in this view were built before 1955. *LT Museum 1541/R.*

Above: Seven pre-war RTs enjoyed a new lease of life between 1955 and 1957, thanks to a bridge at Broxbourne (Hertfordshire) which was too weak to take the weight of standard post-war buses. The older RTs, being 15cwt lighter, came within the weight restrictions imposed on the bridge. So, the seven buses deemed to be in the best condition were painted green and despatched to Hertford Garage where they appeared not just on route 327, which traversed the bridge (strengthened late in 1957) but also on occasions on Hertford's trunk route 310 - taking them right into the busy north London suburb of Enfield. *Bruce Jenkins.*

Right: 1956; 365 days marked and marred by conflict. In the middle east and in eastern Europe there were invasions, fighting and war. In London, the RTs did their duty in rather more stable conditions. Apart from a handful of double-deckers including the prototype Routemaster, which entered trial service in January, they all looked much the same, and the situation wasn't going to alter very much for the next four years. Barking Garage's RTL 341, photographed in Holborn on August 25, is a perfect example of the mid-1950s London bus. There were plenty of other things to take the mind off the international situation; gambling for instance. This was the theme of *Guys and Dolls,* a lavish musical production starring Marlon Brando, Frank Sinatra and Jean Simmons. It was said that the songs were the real stars! If anyone 'fancied a flutter' there was always the pools. Look at all the grinning winners of Vernon's £75,000 'first divi' prize, a King's Ransom back in '56, when an average suburban 'semi' would set you back around £3,000! *Gerald Mead.*

AT HOME

In 1955, which was undoubtedly the heyday year of the RT family, London Transport owned 94 operational bus garages, 63 of them in the central red bus area. Of these, Merton in south London took the prize for providing the biggest Monday to Friday allocation, a total of 181 double-deck buses, all except eight being RTs. The smallest was Abbey Wood with 32 buses, all of them RTs.

Of the 31 country area garages in use in 1955 the largest was Grays in Essex, whose weekday services required 80 RTs. The smallest were East Grinstead and the old Stevenage garage which ran six RTs a piece. Every country area garage operated single deckers in varying quantities. Naturally enough in the 1950s, when most of the photos in this section were taken, almost every London Transport bus garage was playing host to members of the RT family.

Left: A midday scene outside Norwood Garage, in rather grey weather on May 7 1954. The only movement in the picture is provided by the passers-by, all purposefully going about their business. All is still in the bus garage, where a mixture of RTs is waiting for the start of the afternoon peak 'run out'. A notice on the railings on the left reveals that there are vacancies for conductors: the basic weekly wage for a bus conductor in 1954 would have been £7. 8s. 6d (£7.42). This is the old Norwood Garage, which the London General company opened in 1909, just in time for the age of the motor bus. It was closed in April 1981, demolished and rebuilt. The new Norwood bus garage opened for business on October 27 1984. _LT Museum R100._

Above: Barely four miles from Norwood, and in complete contrast, stood Elmers End garage. This was extensively rebuilt following war damage and the work was completed by the end of 1953. Its modern post-war design was similar to several other London Transport garages of the period like Loughton and Romford (North Street). Route 194 had a long association with Elmers End and was part of its daily allocation until October 25 1986, when Elmers End fell victim to late 1980s operating economies; it was closed and demolished. Route 194 is now operated by Croydon Garage. Croydon Airport, RT 3738's destination, closed in 1959, but lives on in many aspects of local life, including the destination of blinds of local buses. _LT Museum 13723._

Top: In north London, Enfield Garage (Ponders End as it is known locally) is still in business. In 1954, the forecourt served as a peak-hour terminus for trolleybus route 627, hence the overhead wires. *LT Museum 5289.*

Above: If there was ever an award for formation parking then the staff at Camberwell must have come close to winning it! On September 14 1954, you could still find a few buses sporting cream upper deck window surrounds. By the mid-50s, bus garages were either AEC or Leyland sheds, at least as far as double deckers were concerned. Camberwell's buses were all Leylands - and RTLs predominated until 1966 when surplus RTs were drafted in to replace them. By then Camberwell was also operating a small number of *Routemasters* on route 40. *LT Museum 1094/4.*

Facing page, lower: Apart from the trolley-bus depots, which eventually became bus garages between 1959 and 1962, the last bus garage to receive RTs was Loughton, in Essex. It did not receive any examples until February 1955, when withdrawal commenced of the last post-war Leyland *Titan* STDs which operated from Loughton. The garage was still fairly new when Saunders-bodied RT 1213 was photographed later in 1955, two years after the premises had been opened to replace a much smaller,

former London General garage, just across the road.
LT Museum H6526.

Below: Another strong contender for a parking prize, this time in diagonal formation, is Uxbridge, the most westerly red bus garage. It was situated just across the Middlesex boundary, in Buckinghamshire. At the other end of the garage, sitting aloof from the RTs in this June 1955 view, is an AEC Regal T-type single decker built

in 1946, and blinded for showing route 222 (Uxbridge Station-London Airport). In 1955, Uxbridge Garage services were 100% outer suburban, but in 1960, when the long 607 trolleybus route was withdrawn, the garage received an allocation on the replacement 207 bus route, and received some brand new *Routemasters*. The old Uxbridge garage closed on December 2 1983, when a large new garage/bus station complex opened, near the tube terminus. *LT Museum 13838.*

Right: In 1954, LT unveiled its 'bus of the future', the *Routemaster*. This all-conquering machine was going to replace London's 1,700-strong trolleybus fleet before making inroads into the RT family. Many years of research and design work had gone into the *Routemaster*, and the fact that in 1989 many examples are still giving excellent service in London and in many towns up and down the country is sufficient testimony to the effort that went into producing it all those years ago. Nevertheless, only a handful of *Routemasters* had come off the production line by early 1959 when LT made a start on ridding London of the silent and pollution-free trolleybuses. So, the first few depots to lose their 'trolleys', like Carshalton and Bexleyheath, in March 1959, received not the RMs that the bus spotters were hoping for, but RTs and RTLs, albeit nicely overhauled, made redundant by bus service reductions the previous year. Gleaming roofbox RT 265, almost 12 years old, stands next to two short wheelbase B1 class trolleybuses in the entrance to Carshalton depot, taking a pounding from a downpour. Carshalton had been home for

the B1s since 1935 and most had spent their entire working lives there on route 654. The replacement bus route was numbered 154, it being LTs policy to use numbers for the new bus routes as similar as possible to the old trolleybus services

they replaced. Thus, a small trolleybus depot became a small bus garage. Further service reductions enabled Carshalton to be closed in January 1964, and today the building is used for storing furniture.
Author's collection.

AT HOME

RT JU

Fifty years of a

The 'RT' bus served London Transport fro
style of those which used to appear in
layout, including fu

ssic London bus

until 1979, and this cutaway view, in the
rs comic *The Eagle,* shows the general
and diesel engine.

MAINTENANCE

BY OPERATING a fleet of buses embodying a high degree of standardisation, in both bodywork and mechanical parts, London Transport was able to introduce a fairly rigid procedure for repairs and maintenance – even if 811 out of the 7,040 scheduled buses in October 1955 were single deckers.

Buses had a routine pattern of maintenance between each overhaul cycle, varying from day-to-day tasks like refuelling, washing and , to the altogether more complex periodic mechanical examinations. Every task from the most minor to the complete overhaul played its own part in keeping the RTs on the road for almost double the generally accepted 15-years life span of most of Britain's buses.

Right: One of the most frequent 'maintenance' jobs carried out on London's buses is the daily wash. Bus washing methods before mechanisation consisted of a basic, labour-intensive hose-down, seen here in practice on a pre-war RT in Victoria Garage in May 1942. *LT Museum 18611.*

Left: Hounslow Garage was extensively modernised in 1955. The new facilities included a steam-clean booth and much less labour-intensive washing equipment, whose spinning brushes moved up and down the bus sides. *LTMuseum 18516.*

Above: Standardisation brought a gradual end to scenes like this, at Victoria Garage in August 1949. There is a good mix of pre-war, wartime and post-war buses receiving attention from the engineers. With the coming of the RT family there were, in many garages, at least ten or more years, and in some cases as many as 20, during which engineers had to cope with maintaining only one type of double-deck bus. In this respect standardisation did not arrive at Victoria Garage until late 1953 when, with the departure of its last STL, all its buses were RTs. In contrast, in 1989, Victoria operates *Routemasters, Metrobuses* and *Midibuses. LT Museum 670.*

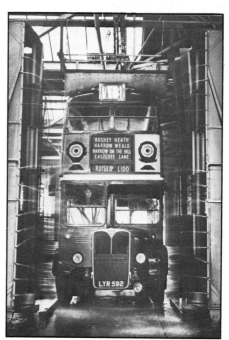

Left: ...The manual hose-down was still being used at Victoria in 1950. From this angle, you can clearly see some of the more subtle curves and tapers of the RT design, not normally visible from pavement level. *LT Museum 11950.*

Right: Another bus washing system made its debut at Harrow Weald garage four years later and was eventually adopted as the standard system. It was fully automatic. When a bus approached the washing booth it broke a beam of light across its path which activated water spray jets. After a thorough dousing, the bus passed under a sponge roller which cleaned the roof before squeezing between two sets of nylon brushes which cleaned the sides. RT 3373 is pictured here during its 'wash and brush up' at Harrow Weald on November 11 1959. The 'target' posters flanking the blinds were among several produced during the late 1950s and early 1960s to entice advertisers to make use of these very eye-catching spaces. Remember "The Eyes Have it" and "Where? Here!"
LT Museum 18433.

MAINTENANCE

Above: The inspection pits at Hounslow Garage, on October 9 1956. Just visible on the side of RT 3585 is its garage code plate. These metal plates proved a popular collectors item amongst schoolboys. The plates were quite easily acquired - you just slid them out of the slots holding them onto the bus, when no one was looking! Who knows, maybe RT 3585's 'AV' plate later found its way into some ink-stained satchel, ready to be swapped for a Dinky racing car or some back numbers of the Dandy! This reprehensible activity prompted London Transport to adopt a policy of stencilling garage codes onto its buses from about 1960. *LT Museum 17492.*

Right: To passengers, a bus with a clean and tidy interior is probably more important than glossy paintwork outside, and over the years many methods have been tried to make bus cleaning both easier and quicker. This system, in use at Mortlake Garage in April 1962, involved the use of high pressure jets.
LT Museum R2803.

COUNTRY GARAGES

THE GARAGES in London Transport's Country Area were operated in much the same way as those which worked red buses. As the years pass, and even London Country Bus Services Ltd (the company which took over LTs green bus region on January 1 1970) is dismantled and sold, the memory of bright red and dark green RTs running on the same streets in outer London towns like Watford, Croydon, Kingston and Romford, begins to fade.

These suburban towns were the 'front doors' to London Transport's Country Area, shaped like a tyre around the hub of the nation's capital city.

As a country bus, the RT performed as well as it did in city traffic, especially in its provision of increased capacity on routes serving the ever-expanding New Towns during the '50s and early '60s. Although the quiet villages and country lanes of London's countryside are more usually associated with single deckers, it was never a surprise to see dark green RTs in remote places like Hedgerley, Coxtie Green, Faygate and Farleigh. The Country Area services were planned so that the busier trips on many established single-deck routes could be covered by double-deckers scheduled to coincide with school or factory finishing times.

There were approximately 775 green-liveried RTs scheduled for service during the mid-1950s, the number varying subsequently to meet changing traffic requirements. In January 1970, London Country took over 484 green RTs from LT, all that remained in service by the end of 1969, and operated them in rapidly diminishing numbers until the last example was withdrawn during September 1978.

Right: There was some overlap between London Transport's Central and Country Bus areas and Leatherhead garage, with its typical '30s style offices (complete with 'bullseye' pole on top) provided one of the most southerly points on the red bus map. For many years it served as the terminus for route 65, and later the 71. Here, on a sultry August day in 1955, RT 3101 from Norbiton garage waits to begin the 15-miles journey north to Ealing, taking it through some of the most picturesque riverside scenery around London. Behind is a green RT, one of the 59 buses required to run Leatherhead's Monday-Friday schedules at the time, 'blinded' for route 416 (Leatherhead-Esher). In 1955, the 416 service required only one bus to operate its daily schedule. What a contrast to the 46 buses needed for the 65! The critics didn't go into raptures over _Daddy Longlegs_, although Fred Astaire's dancing was apparently up to its usual standard. _LT Museum U57962._

Left: Romford Garage never operated a country bus route, only the high frequency Green Line services 721 and 722. Nevertheless, the forecourt was used until the garage closed, and for sometime after, as the terminus for Grays route 370. London Road, Romford looked unusually quiet when visited by the LT photographer on August 10 1955. The garage was formerly owned by the independent Hillman's Saloon Coaches, becoming part of Green Line on January 10 1934. It was extensively rebuilt in 1973/4, only to be closed in 1977 when the 721 service was withdrawn. In common with many other former bus garages it is now a DIY Superstore. _LT Museum U57912._

Top: Many of the country area garages were smaller than those in the red bus area. This was not always a problem, but in a few cases changing circumstances rendered some of the older garages obsolete. By the 1950s several new towns had appeared on the London environs map, Harlow Stevenage, Crawley and Hemel Hempstead among them. A network of new bus routes grew in and around the new towns and these in turn needed larger premises to accommodate the buses required. Some completely new garages were built, while others were enlarged. There were some casualties too, like homely little Hatfield garage, pictured here on August 10 1955, complete with placards advertising special Green Line excursions to London or beyond. The garage accommodated 29 buses, 25 of them RTs. They ran on six different routes and between them covered some 4,000 miles a day. The routes served nearby Hatfield, Welwyn Garden City and the rapidly expanding Stevenage new town. By the late 1950s Hatfield garage had become inadequate. *LT Museum U57914.*

Right: A new Hatfield Garage was built and was opened on February 18 1959, by Alderman E. J. Baxter, then Chairman of Hertfordshire County Council. It was as spacious as the old garage was cramped: the new under-cover accommodation housed 49 buses, and there was plenty of room around its perimeter to stand a few more. The administration block stood apart from the main garage area, adjacent to the main St. Albans Road. *LT Museum 14520.*

Left: Inside, Hatfield garage was all 'mod con.' It was the first LT garage to be built on a framework of tubular steel erected in spans 100ft across, with no centre support structure. It utilised all the latest engineering equipment and facilities, including three inspection pits fitted with fluorescent lighting. *LT Museum 14717.*

Left: As the new Hatfield garage opened, work was finishing, just a few miles to the north, on yet another new base for country buses. This was the new Stevenage garage, which also had room for 49 buses, two of which are seen standing, by the main entrance, soon after the premises opened for business in April 1959. The single-deck RF is seemingly not engaged on anything in particular, but RT 4167 is 'blinded' for town service 801. The 800 series of country bus routes began life on March 3 1954, specifically to cater for the expansion of services in the new towns. The 801 was the first such route to be introduced and before 1959 was operated from the small Hitchin garage, four miles to the north west, another casualty of the opening of the new Hatfield and Stevenage garages. *LT Museum 9437.*

Above: One of the largest of all the country bus garages was Garston, in north Watford, which for many years operated far fewer buses than its spacious area could accommodate. In 1952, only 60 buses were scheduled to run from there on weekdays, but by the end of the decade this had risen to 111 - and all but 15 were RTs. Back in July 1952, a still fairly new RT 3458, pauses for refuelling after a stint on route 351 (Uxbridge-Harpenden) which was later merged into trunk route 321. Behind is a post-war T-type single-decker also awaiting fuel. *LT Museum H16911.*

COUNTRY GARAGES

ALDENHAM WORKS

ONE of the many advantages in operating a large, standardised bus fleet like the RT family was that economies of scale could be given full reign. What better example can be given of economies of scale in this context than Aldenham Works which, by 1956, was the world's largest bus overhaul factory? It was fully equipped to give every standard London bus a thorough overhaul every three and a half to four years.

London Transport was aware from an early date that such a task was not possible at Chiswick Works, where bus overhauling had been hitherto carried out. So, when the awesome prospect of thousands of standard buses in its fleet was no longer merely an ambition, it set about finding a suitable site on which to build the premises to carry out the mammoth task of mass overhauling. But before a site was found, and to give Chiswick some temporary relief, LT diverted some bus maintenance work to the new but unfinished Northern Line train depot in the village of Aldenham near Elstree in Hertfordshire. The depot was being built in anticipation of the Underground being extended north of Edgware.

When plans for the tube extension were finally abandoned in September 1949, London Transport settled on Aldenham as the site for its bus overhaul factory. Between 1952 and 1955, work continued on building and equipping the plant, and by the end of 1955 Aldenham was well into the task of turning out over 45 newly-overhauled buses each week. With the official opening of Aldenham in October 1956, it could be said that London Transport had realised all the targets it had set when the RT project was first conceived: it had designed and produced a standardised bus for London and provided facilities for both small and large scale maintenance work to be performed.

Above: Aldenham Works, in its day the largest passenger service vehicle overhaul factory in the world. This view shows the works in 1956, the year it was officially opened by the Minister of Transport, Harold Watkinson. The picture clearly illustrates the scale of the plant; the floor space covered 17 acres and the main building was some 480 yards in length. The buses in the forecourt are pre-war RTs which, following their withdrawal from service the previous year, found employment as staff buses ferrying those of the 1,800 Aldenham employees without their own transport home to all four corners of the LT area. Aldenham Works didn't alter much in the 30 or so years between this view and December 1987 when the factory, much slimmed down and having to pitch for bus overhaul work with outside companies, closed its giant doors for the last time. *LT Museum 24569.*

Left: Early days at Aldenham, before the works flow process got under way. Nearest the camera are spare RT bodies mounted on blocks, to provide an overhaul 'float.' At the far end of the shop is a mixture of pre-war buses receiving mechanical and cosmetic attention, and just visible on the right is one of two special 8ft wide test rig buses built to survey routes to determine their suitability to take RTWs. *London Trolleybus Preservation Society.*

Above, left: During the period before London Transport decided to base its giant bus overhaul works at Aldenham, the works, then still officially an embryo tube train depot, was used for bus maintenance and checking new buses as they were delivered. One such is brand new RT 1125, which was in the works on February 17 1949, a few days before it entered service from Muswell Hill garage, where it helped to oust six-wheeler AEC Renown LT type double deckers from route 43, many nearing 20 years old. *LT Museum U46150.*

Above, right: When Aldenham became fully operational, many of the chassis components were overhauled at Chiswick, after which parts were sent back to Aldenham for reassembly. To ensure maximum efficiency, the chassis overhaul shop at Aldenham was immediately adjacent to the body repair bays, so that no time was lost when it came to reuniting body and chassis. *LT Museum 21614.*

Above: By late 1955, Aldenham was giving full overhauls to the RT family using procedures planned for maximum efficiency. The first thing that happened to a bus entering Aldenham was the separation of its body from its chassis, which was then dismantled. The body was then subjected to a thorough inspection with all damaged panels and fittings being marked for replacement. *LT Museum 14232.*

Left: The body was then tilted over as shown here and the underside given a high pressure wash to remove all traces of dirt, oil and grease accumulated during the preceding period of active service, usually 180 weeks. *LT Museum 18686*

Left: Bodies for repair were then moved to the standing area, where the panelling was repaired, either using new or reconditioned parts. Movement of bus bodies along the huge body shop was by an overhead gantry. *LT Museum 16581.*

ALDENHAM WORKS

Right: At the other end of the shop, the body (complete with all its new parts) was remounted onto a chassis which itself had been completely overhauled. The more standard Park Royal or Weymann bodies could be mounted onto either AEC or Leyland chassis, but the Craven and Metro Cammell bodies were kept within their respective AEC or Leyland batches. The Saunders bodies were only ever fitted to AECs. Here a Metro Cammell body is manoeuvred back onto an RTL chassis of the same batch from which it was taken a few days earlier. *LT Museum 14233*

Below: After the reunion of chassis and body, an overhauled bus (devoid of seat cushions and looking like patchwork of red or green and primer) underwent stringent riding and braking tests on Aldenham's perimeter road. Then it was into the paint shop. Before the undercoat was dry the top coat of gloss was applied, followed by two coats of varnish. RT bodies may have had five or more overhauls during their working lives and some even changed colour from red to green, or vice versa, depending on the fleet requirement at the time. This RTL is emerging from the paint booth in red livery. *LT Museum 1407/23.*

Below: One of the novel features at Aldenham was the tilt test, which every bus had to undergo before going back to work. The object was to ensure that each bus could tilt to a maximum of 30 degrees without toppling over. as demonstrated by RT 919, following its overhaul in July 1960. *LT Museum 21021.*

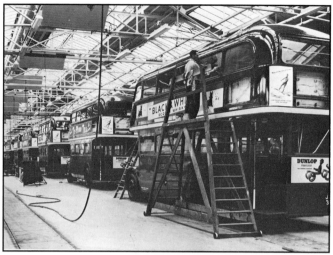

Above: After painting, varnishing and drying the bus received its new identity. It was most unlikely that a bus would receive the same stock number it lost on entering the works 15 days before, but for a time London Transport ensured that its 'ambassador buses', those which had been on goodwill trips abroad, received the same body after overhaul. Bus licensing procedure made it more sensible to allocate to an overhauled vehicle a stock/registration number from a bus newly-arrived for repair at Aldenham. This ensured continuity of the road tax. Thus, if Hendon garage sent RT 2217 to Aldenham for overhaul on a Monday, it was quite likely that a newly-overhauled bus carrying the number RT 2217 could be waiting to re-enter service somewhere else. Indeed, it has been known for two buses with identical numbers to be in the same garage at the same time, one newly arrived from Aldenham, the other about to go there for overhaul. What a nightmare for the bus spotter! Here, an RTL brings up the rear of a line of completed buses on the finishing line. Newly re-covered seat swabs have been fitted, adverts posted, transfers applied. Like a new bus, this RTL is about to begin another three and a half to four year stint as one of the best cared for passenger carriers in the world. *LT Museum 16580.*

Left, below: Wallop! One of the jobs undertaken at Aldenham was the repair of buses damaged in accidents, like the unhappy consequences of taking a wrong turning and running under a low bridge. The hapless driver of RT 1420 may be unaware that his momentary lapse of concentration has an important place in the history of the RT, for although the Craven-built body was not considered worth repairing and was scrapped, the chassis was subsequently mounted with the original body carried by RT 1. The resulting vehicle became a mobile instruction bus in LTs service fleet. In 1979, re-registered EYK 396, the bus was carefully restored to 1939 splendour by the late Prince Marshall with original livery and advertisements. It appeared at Barking for the last RT day celebrations on April 7, and subsequently at various open days that year, which was also the 150th anniversary of Shilibeer's original Omnibus, the first London bus of all. RT 1 was subsequently sold to an American buyer, but was back in the UK in 1989, just in time for its 50th birthday party. *J.C. Gilliam.*

ALDENHAM WORKS

BUS STATIONS

Below: Passengers board brand new RT 2270 at Morden bus station on September 3 1949. It was always LT policy to build bus termini adjacent to railway stations where possible, and Morden had been a model of this practice since the 'tube' opened in 1926. RT 2270 was one of a number of green RTs delivered new to the Central Area in 1949 to cover red bus shortages. A large new office block was built above Morden station in the 1960s. *Alan B. Cross*.

Right: One place you would imagine would have a proper bus station is Waterloo, where thousands of commuters arrive by train each working day. Well, think again, because Waterloo doesn't have a focal point for boarding buses. Instead, there are a number of different stops in the area depending on the route you want to use. In the early 1950s, commuters board rather shabby RTL 432, which is taking on passengers travelling north to Aldwych and beyond. Some may have been intending to visit the National Handicrafts and Hobbies Exhibition at Central Hall, Westminster, entrance to which was one silver shilling (5p). The rear platform advertisement space on London's buses has always been an ideal location to 'reach' the motorist. *LT Museum 4598.*

Above: In complete contrast, Victoria station has a large adjacent bus terminus. It had hardly changed in more than 30 years when this view was taken on June 10 1957. The route number stops are still set in the original GENERAL posts and many of the services are using the same parking bays as they have for years. Since 1968, Victoria Bus Station has been under cover. Routes 16, 25, 38 and 52 still terminate there. In 1957, route 25 had the distinction of requiring the largest single allocation of buses from any one garage - 69 RTs from Forest Gate weekdays, augmented by six RTLs from Clay Hall. But things were already in decline, for in 1950 Forest Gate's weekday total on the 25 service had been a colossal 81 RTs, with Clay Hall supplying eight RTLs. Today, after surviving many intermediate route changes route 25 still runs, as it did for many years, from Victoria to Becontree Heath. The Monday-Friday allocation is 53 Leyland Titans from Bow Garage, which was a thriving trolleybus depot back in 1957, when this picture was taken.
LT Museum 18558.

Left: One London bus station which has changed considerably since it was visited by London Transport's photographer on October 20 1957 is London Bridge; the main line station has been rebuilt and buses now stand under cover. The 1957 petrol rationing following the Suez crisis created an unexpected financial bonus for LT as it brought many additional passengers. It was a leading factor in the organisation paying its way that year for the first time since 1948. However, by October, petrol rationing had ended. People had returned to their cars and traffic congestion was causing serious problems. LT was pressing the authorities to bring in measures to restrict parking in central London and carry out road improvements at bottlenecks like the north side of London Bridge which RTW 461 on route 8A, and the two RTs on the 43 service will have to negotiate soon after their journeys from the bus station begin.
LT Museum 17754.

Above, left: The scene at Hounslow Bus station on September 9 1956, probably around mid-day. The bus is still very much in command, and its position will strengthen in the coming months as a political crisis in the Suez Canal develops and eventually leads to nationwide petrol rationing. Maybe the people by the news-stand are discussing Suez as they wait for their bus. Clapham garage's RTL 1079 was possibly the first one to leave the ter-minus on the long suburban route 37

which will take it right across south west and south London. *LT Museum 1424/1.*

Above, right: For many years there were no proper parking bays at Golders Green bus station - the only guide for drivers were the road markings in the forecourt. Film 'buffs' will easily tell the year this picture was taken because two sixties British classics, Alfie and Morgan (A suit-able case for treatment) are advertised on

the buses. It's 1966, May 10 to be precise. Bus 'buffs' will tell you that the RT family was just four days away from losing one of its valued members: on Saturday May 14 the last of the 8ft wide RTWs was with-drawn, from Walworth garage. The RTs/-RTL in the view are joined by *Routemas-ters* working on route 13, a Green Line coach *Routemaster* (RMC) at the back of the bus park, and a red AEC Regal RF single decker on route 210.
LT Museum 2456.

TO THE AIRPORT

The RT had a long association with London Airport, but the first ordinary bus route to actually terminate at Heathrow did not start running until 1954. This followed the opening of the new tunnel, which took traffic

beneath the runways right into the main terminal area. RTs continued to serve the airport until 1978, when passengers flying in on the most tech-nically advanced airliners to the world's busiest international airport

could complete their journeys (assuming their destination was Greenford or Harrow) on a 30-years old RT, examples of which were still running right into the airport complex on routes 105 and 140.

Right: The new tunnel into 'London Airport' opened in 1953. At Heathrow on October 3 that year, with the builders putting the fin-ishing touches to the portal, RT 2318 takes a party of visitors to inspect the new facility and the central enclo-sure beyond.
LT Museum 4650.

Left: This obviously posed shot was taken to publicise the start of London Transport's new weekend route 81B, run for the benefit of sightseers from Hounslow to what was described as the 'Central Enclosure' at Heathrow. For the purpose, RT1619 was taken to an airport, possibly Northolt, and photographed with a USAF C54 plane. *LT Museum U56350.*

Below: Heathrow is growing, and more bus routes are serving the area. Twickenham Garage's RT 2213 passes the giant hangars near Hatton Cross outside which are two piston-engined Boeing 377 Stratocruisers. The date is March 6 1958, the year before the last 377s flew for BOAC. A Vauxhall *Wyvern* brings up the rear as the bus, which in common with the rest of the RT family, has had its attractive polished wheel hubs painted over in the drab red oxide paint used for the rest of the wheel. *LT Museum 17008.*

Left: Ten years on from the days of the *Stratocruiser*, and the BOAC fleet is operating VC10s in its passenger fleet. On the road, London Transport is still happily operating RTs, one of which is dwarfed by the distinctive tails of a couple of VC10s on the Perimeter Road. *LT Museum 440/1310/D.*

TO THE AIRPORT

FARES PLEASE

Below, left: In the early post-war period, LT carried out experiments with 'Pay As You Board' buses, not on today's driver-only principle, but with passengers paying their fares to a seated conductor who no longer had to move around the bus. One of the buses used extensively in the trials was pre-war RT 97, which had suffered bomb damage and needed rebuilding. It was fitted with rear doors, and in the area formerly occupied by the nearside longitudinal seat, sat the conductor at a counter complete with cash register. RT 97's platform area was enlarged by repositioning the staircase further inside the bus and this enabled up to 20 passengers to stand inside while waiting to pay their fares as the bus moved away from the stop. RT 97 entered service in its new form on route 65 from Kingston garage in January 1946. In March it was repainted in Green Line colours and was sent to Romford Garage, where it worked on route 721. The bus is seen here loading passengers at Aldgate bus station on May 22 1946. *LT Museum 16324.*

Below, right: The PAYB experiment was a failure, mainly because of boarding delays, especially when more passengers than the platform could accommodate wanted to board. Problems were experienced with the cash machines too. A look inside RT97 shows the modifications carried out to accommodate the conductor's position. *LT Museum 16322.*

Right, upper: PAYB was a brief and novel diversion for a single RT; for the rest of the family, fare collection was carried out, as it always had been, by a conductor or conductress, who moved around the bus taking fares and dispensing tickets. For the first few years of the RT, traditional Bell Punch tickets were issued. The Bell Punch system, with the conductor carrying a rack of tickets of different fare denominations, and wearing a cancellor strapped to the tunic, had been a feature of London's buses since the 1890s. It is seen in use in October 1952 in the capable hands of a 'clippie' wearing a rather austere grey lightweight coat. *LT Museum 24562.*

Right, lower: In 1953, LT unveiled its new paper-roll ticket machine. It was called 'The Gibson', after its inventor, George Gibson, the Superintendent of LT's Effra Road ticket machine works. Over the next five years 'Gibsons,' as well as other machines based on the roll paper principle replaced all the Bell Punch machines on London's buses and trolleybuses. This one is dispensing tickets on May 11 1956. The man with the newspaper might be reading about the mysterious disappearance of Royal Navy frogman Commander Crabb (sic), who had been diving near a Russian ship the *Ordzhonikdze* which had brought two high ranking Russians, Nikita Kruschchev and Nikolai Bulganin, on a visit to Britain. Or he may be intrigued by a review of a new play which had opened in at London's Royal Court Theatre that week. It was John Osborne's *Look Back In Anger* about post-war frustrations of the young. The era of 'kitchen sink' dramas had dawned. *LT Museum 20200.*

Above: Following its unsuccessful role in the PAYB experiments London Transport rebuilt RT 97 as an experimental Green Line coach, and gave it the code RTC 1, an only child for the RT family. RTC 1 was finished early in 1949 and, as this early posed photograph taken at an LT sports ground in February that year shows, its design especially the engine cover) was very advanced for the time. It had no opening windows so it had to be fully air conditioned. It also boasted fluorescent lighting - very new in 1949. Regular Green Line users didn't like RTC1 very much, for it was 'stuffy' inside, also there was nowhere to deposit luggage. LT, confident about the reliability of the air conditioning, allowed smoking on both decks. The bus ran in Green Line service until the end of 1949 when it was demoted as an ordinary country bus. It was withdrawn in 1953 and sold to Vernons Pools in Liverpool, who used it with some pride as a staff bus. *LT Museum 16422.*

INCLEMENT WEATHER

WIND, rain, fog, flood, ice and snow, bad weather, although a fact of British life, has been known to paralyse even parts of central London let alone the suburbs and home counties. Public transport has an obligation to operate the best service it can in all weathers, and during its 40 year span, the RT family encountered and endured its share of the worst, and some of the best, weather recorded in the second half of the century. For example, to accompany the bad winters of 1946/7 and 1962, there were the sweltering summers of 1959 and 1976 – and the jubilee summer of 1989 was also very hot as this book went to press.

Left: Thick fog and, worse still, smog, (a mixture of smoke and fog) appeared regularly during autumns and winters until the clean air legislation of the early 1960s banished them for good. Known as 'pea soupers,' for the young they usually meant an early finish to school and a walk home with a scarf over nose and mouth. For those trying to keep public services moving, smog was a nightmare. Here, an Inspector leading RT 268 through the murk in Commercial Road in November 1952 is using a flaming torch to assist a safe journey. *LT Museum H17167.*

Snow makes much prettier pictures! In April 1950, an unusually large unseasonal snowfall brought havoc to the roads and weighed heavy on the spring bulbs and blossom. In this Christmas card view, workmen are clearing away the remains of a fallen tree near Croydon as RT 1579, one of the few motor vehicles to venture out it seems, gingerly edges past. *Author's collection.*

Above, left: The raked-back front of the RT made an excellent snow trap, and any bus which had been left outside in a blizzard soon had its destination screen obliterated by the white flakes. The snow is gradually thawing from the front of green RT 609 as it pulls away from a stop in Brookmans Park on February 7 1969, and soon it would slide off completely, probably startling the driver in the process. *J.G.S. Smith.*

Above, right: There was a particularly harsh winter in 1962/63, with plenty of snow, and London's bus services, especially those which ran across exposed areas like the 93 service on Wimbledon Common, were badly disrupted. In this scene, RT 908's red livery doubtless provided a welcome splash of bright colour in the bleak winter landscape.
LT Museum H16913.

A QUESTION OF CONGESTION

Above, left: A classic car jam - 1960s style. Let's not dwell too much on the cause and effect of traffic delays, no-one can take any pleasure from them, least of all LT which progressively lost more bus mileage as a result of road delays from the 1950s onwards. Two buses are caught here in Finchley Road, a single-deck Private Hire RF coach, and an RT on route 113. The date is July 1961, and the shot is full of nostalgia. Can you name all the makes of car in the line? If not, no matter. They are almost all of British origin with long forgotten names like Sunbeam, Hillman, Riley, Wolsley and Morris. A similar jam in Finchley Road, or anywhere, today would be composed of Nissans, Renaults, Toyotas, BMWs and Peugeots. The delays are still the same but the component parts have changed, that's all. *LT Museum 21494.*

Above, right: Even by 1955, LT was attempting to meet the challenges of the private car by introducing what would today be called 'innovative services'. In 1955 this was an 'express' version of an established route connecting a predominantly residential area with a nearby major town. The first express route linked the large estate at New Addington with Croydon, four miles to the north. The journey could be made by conventional bus route 130 but on August 10 1955, LT introduced a limited stop service on the same route. It was run with ordinary RTs distinguished by white on blue destination and number blinds proclaiming 'EXPRESS'. Other routes, including the 174 in the Romford area, followed suit with an express service, and the principle is still used today, the 130 express journeys now being numbered X30. On the first day, Croydon garage's newly overhauled RT 956 traverses the New Addington estate with an 'all stops' 130 behind. How many of its passengers had been tempted away from their cars by the promise of a quick ride into Croydon, with no parking problems? *LT Museum 52475.*

Right: Petrol rationing resulting from the crisis in the Suez canal was in force between December 1956 and May 1957. Although it had some detrimental effect on bus services (some higher fares were charged and some off-peak journeys withdrawn) buses generally benefited from the situation with additional patrons and relatively empty streets. This view of Bank in March 1957 illustrates the point, but unfortunately the time of day is not recorded. However, RTW 269 (leading) with RTL 599 behind have the road almost to themselves. *LT Museum 1455/6.*

Above: This is BESI, London's first mechanical attempt to keep a track on the position of buses on busy routes. BESI stood for Bus Electronic Scanning Indicator: every time a BESI bus passed a special roadside post, a 'magic eye' would 'read' the bus identification contained in a plate slotted into the side of the vehicle. The information was relayed to a controller who could see at a glance where every bus on the route was; if they were bunching together, he would brief a roadside inspector to take remedial action. Here, RTW 498 demonstrates the new system. The bus is carrying the famous 'Hop On A Bus' posters, part of a campaign by LT to encourage people to make use of their buses once again after the 1958 strike. *LT Museum 1713/3.*

THE 1958 STRIKE

EVEN today, commuters of the era still talk about the 1958 London bus strike, not so much because of the inconvenience it caused, for like the effect of similar strikes involving transport, that is soon forgotten. The 1958 stoppage is remembered more because it is nowadays widely regarded as being influential in creating the style of bus services which we have today. There are other factors of course, but between May 4 and June 21 1958 many people learned to live without their buses and some never went back to them.

Above, left: Like most strikes the 1958 Bus Strike was over pay and conditions. This view at the bottom of Charing Cross Road shows the chaotic effect it had: cars, private hire coaches and pedestrians all jostling for space. *LT Museum 21755.*

Above right: By the end of 1958, LT had withdrawn 20 bus routes and pruned sections of, or reduced the service frequency on many others. One casualty was the short 239 route which connected Romford with Gidea Park. It set down its last passengers on Tuesday August 19. RT 340 and the 239 service may have gone, but Ty Phoo tea and Heinz salad cream are both still with us today. *Bruce Jenkins.*

Left: A huge quantity of buses were made redundant in the wake of the service reductions, and many were offered for sale. Here at Avonmouth Docks, some of the unwanted RTs and RTLs are loaded onto a steamer for Ceylon (now Sri Lanka) where they were to give as much as 20 years further service. It is strange to think that when this picture was taken, LT still had a quantity of hitherto new but unused RTs languishing in its garages waiting to earn their first penny in passenger service. *Author's collection.*

TWO DECADES OF DECLINE

THE DESCRIPTION 'Two decades of decline' makes the situation sound worse than it was, but that in effect is how long it took London Transport to dispose of the RT family. At first, the decline was so slow as to be almost unnoticeable, but by the end of 1962 it was gathering momentum. By 1968, when the last of the *Routemasters* entered service, almost all the Leyland RTs had been withdrawn. Then it was the turn of the Merlins, *Swifts, Fleetlines* and *Routemasters* made redundant by their arrival, to oust the remaining RTs, 3,556 of which were still in service in September 1968. Additionally, bus service levels were still being adversely affected by the continuing growth of private transport, many people preferring to have a 'tiger in their tank' (to quote a famous Esso petrol advert of the day) to a bus ticket in their pocket.

Above, left: The telephoto lens emphasises the eclipse of the RT by the *Routemaster,* in this evocative view. RT 4186 tags along behind its successor, both having just crossed Westminster Bridge, in June 1965. At the time. the last of the 27ft 6in *Routemasters* had been delivered and the first of the 30ft lengthened versions of the bus were in production. 1965 was the year of LT's controversial Bus Reshaping Plan which prophesied the end of the traditional crew-operated London busin favour of a network of satellite flat-fare routes around strategic shopping and residential centres. Any surviving crew-operated buses would be found only on the busy trunk routes. To an extent the Plan has come true, and its implementation is still under way, a quarter of a century later. *LT Museum 21445.*

Above, right: Towards the end of 1959, LT's Central Bus Department suffered a shortage of red RTs. More were needed to augment AEC requirements in central garages affected by the conversion from trolleybus to diesel bus. To provide the additional AECs, the Country Department agreed to donate 18 of its RTs in exchange for a similar number of RTLs which were painted green in October 1959 - the first and last RTLs to carry this colour. These buses were allocated to Hatfield garage, but the Country Department had a tough job persuading the drivers and engineers to accept them. Finally, in July 1960 the green RTLs did enter service, but within a year the last had been withdrawn, replaced by a freshly-painted batch of green RTs displaced by the delivery of new *Routemasters*. If the schoolboy, in the picture, perhaps a bus 'buff', is considering asking the driver how he thinks the RTL handles compared to the customary AEC, he may well have found himself on the receiving end of some choice language! *Alan B. Cross.*

Above, left: The *Cutty Sark* at Greenwich is a popular destination for Londoners and visitors alike. Since the opening of the Docklands Light Railway in 1987 it's been easier to reach Greenwich from north of the river; just a short walk through the pedestrian tunnel and you're there. Back in 1962, when RTL 1501 was photographed on route 185, it took a little longer to get to the *Cutty Sark* and the other maritime attractions in SE10, especially from the north. The *Cutty Sark* was still a fairly

new attraction in 1962, having only been resident in its own dry dock since 1954. *LT Museum 18660.*

Above, right: Eltham Well Hall Station is a good starting point for a bus ride into suburban Kent, a territory which, as far as buses go, has changed a great deal since these two roof-box RTs were photographed back in 1964. These days, with many of the area's bus routes having gone through the rigors of sevice tendering,

you would be hard put to find a red bus in the area. Routes 61 and 228 are in the hands of other operators in 1989. In 1964, it was rare to find one of the early post-war RTs, represented here by RT 862, on the left. The last of these distinctive buses, recognisable by the fairing strip below the canopy, was withdrawn in May the following year. RT 4798, on the right, has a later type of roof box body, examples of which were still in service as late as 1970. *Alan B. Cross.*

Above, left: Most people will probably have heard of the Dartford Tunnel, which features almost daily on radio road delay reports. When it opened on November 18 1963, it was just a two-way tunnel under the Thames. Today, it links the northern and southern section of the M25 orbital motorway around London, but back in 1963 LT made sure that anyone wanting to take advantage of this new subterranean Essex-Kent link had the opportunity to make the journey by bus. New bus route 300 was introduced, linking Grays with

Dartford on the Kent side, and Green Line route 722 was extended through the tunnel to Dartford as well. In 1963, LT was levied six shillings (30p) each time a bus went through the tunnel toll gate. Sixpence (2.5p) was added to each adult fare in an attempt to recoup the money. The services were not successful. RT 2729 emerges into the Kentish daylight on April 10 1964. *LT Museum 172291.*

Above, right: Once in Dartford, it would have been a convenient change from the

300 service to a 480 route, for a trip through industrial north Kent to Gravesend. There you'd encounter the local bus services, like the 498 service from Northfleet to the Painters Ash Estate in Gravesend. On September 24 1964, red-liveried RT 4183 was working on the route. There were many occasions when the central department loaned RTs to the country area to cover temporary shortages. The bus is stopped near Gravesend Clock Tower, one of the landmarks of the town. *L.W. Rowe.*

TWO DECADES OF DECLINE

Right, upper: When Stockwell garage was built in 1952, it had the distinction of possessing the largest expanse of unsupported concrete roof anywhere in Europe. The roof, which survives today, provided shelter to RTLs until the mid-sixties, the last being replaced by RMs in May 1967. In this 1965 view, a few of Stockwell's RTLs stand in a corner of the garage awaiting the start of the next busy period. *Author's collection.*

Right, lower: The rolling Buckinghamshire landscape to the north of High Wycombe dwarfs green RT4174 as it climbs steep Totteridge Hill at the back of the town in 1969. This was LT's last year as a provider of bus services to the towns and villages around London. The term 'Town Service' wouldn't give much guidance to a stranger to High Wycombe and yet similar 'via' blinds were commonly used, especially on buses in the new towns. This apart, any reader who has persevered this far will surely agree that the RT family must without question win the award for providing the most comprehensive blind information ever carried on London buses. *J.G.S. Smith.*

Below: Denton, the most easterly point served by LT south of the Thames, provided the terminus for the long route 480, which connected Gravesend with Erith, 12 miles away. Denton seems a good place to build up one's strength before the start of a lengthy bus ride - a pub and a fish and chip shop are close by to sustain the inner man! The 480 service was running a 10-minute interval service in May 1965 when RT 989 was photographed turning at Denton.
L.W. Rowe.

Left, top: The RT ended its days in the London suburbs, amid shopping parades, local stations, parks and 'semis.' The enemy of the RT in outer London was the driver-only single deckers, the AEC *Merlins* and *Swifts*, and route 252 in Havering fell victim to the latter in March 1971. Two RTs are seen meeting at the South Hornchurch terminus of the 252, RT 2770 pulling away as 2295 arrives. *J.G.S. Smith.*

Left: Route 146 was probably the most picturesque of LTs red bus routes still utilising RTs in the 1970s. It meandered down from Bromley, through Hayes, across Keston Common to the village of Downe. The practice of advertising pop albums on buses had begun by 1975. *The Rubettes*, who were in the charts that week with *I can do it,* adorn the front target spaces of the RT, a far cry indeed from the marmalade, biscuits and soft drinks of two decades earlier! *John Reed.*

Left, lower: Every aspiring bus driver has to undergo a period of vigorous training before being allowed to take the wheel of a public service vehicle, and until 1985 London Transport maintained a skid patch at its giant Chiswick Works in west London. On its slippery surface, new recruits had to demonstrate that they could control a London bus on icy, wet, or oily roads should the situation arise. An obsolete bus was usually used as the resident skid bus, and on August 12 1975 RT 2189 was in the role. The skid pan was right in front of the Training Manager's Office at Chiswick - and this was surely sufficient incentive to prevent any trainee driver from approaching the skid too fast and hurtling the seven and a half tonner right through his window. *John Reed.*

Right: The RT's foothold is still strong in this November 18 1969 view at Piccadilly Circus; six of the eight buses in sight here are RTs, but the 'family' is no more, for the few Leylands left in LTs fleet were on driver training duties. Nearest the camera is an AEC Merlin *Red Arrow* single decker, similar to the buses which were at the time being used to convert many of London's bus routes to driver-only operation. Completing the team is a lone *Routemaster* on route 53. The 'swinging sixties', of which London was the capital, had just six weeks left to run. The confused and downbeat '70s were just around the corner. The 1960s will be remembered for its music revolution, and at the top of the charts on November 18 1969 were The Archies singing *Sugar Sugar*, but not far behind were names more readily associated with the era, The Hollies, Bob Dylan, Joe Cocker and Mama Cass. All this was a far cry indeed from the world which the roof box RT emerging from Shaftesbury Avenue was built to serve in the late 1940s, when favourite singers included Frankie Laine, Peggy Lee, and Perry Como. *LT Museum 12794-7.*

Above, left: Leytonstone's chief claim to fame is that it was the birthplace of the film director Alfred Hitchcock, but for those who know the area, the names Green Man, Bearmans and Rialto conjure the locality immediately. The Green Man public house overlooks the bus terminus where many routes, particularly those from the Essex suburbs, end their journeys. The terminus is rather remote from the shops in Leytonstone High Road, which for many years boasted one of east London's finest department stores, Bearmans. The store has now gone but was still in business in May 1976 when this line of RTs could be seen at the Green Man, headed by Loughton's RT 2268. Route 148 is note-

worthy in that in 1989 it still follows much the same path as it did when it was introduced way back in February 1926.
John Reed.

Above, right: One of the hilliest routes in the red bus area must have been the 261 service, which ran from Arnos Grove to Barnet. It was introduced on June 21 1961 and was worked by RTs from the outset. On August 30 1977, RT 2399 bounds up Church Hill Road towards Palmers Green. What a pity the picture cannot convey the throbbing growl of the engine as the bus makes the ascent! *John Reed.*

Above, left: Against a backdrop of undulating Essex landscape, looking over towards Loughton, stands Lambourne End and The Camelot public house. For many years The Camelot, or The Beehive as it was once called, provided a terminus for red bus route 26 which ran down to Ilford Station via Grange Hill. The 26 was a casualty of the 1958 bus strike, after which the Lambourne End journeys were tacked on to route 150. Route 101 also ran on from Wanstead to Lambourne End as a summer extension for many years. In 1973, LT withdrew the weekend service to Lambourne End, the only time it was ever really used, and the hamlet had to be satisfied with just a few journeys on weekdays. When the 150 was converted to driver-only operation in October 1977 the Camelot journeys were withdrawn altogether. On

October 7, a week before the sad event, RT 2929 stands in splen-did isolation at Lambourne End, waiting to return to Ilford.
John Reed.

Above, right: In true 'last tram' style, the final day of RTs at Bromley and Catford garages in August 1978 brought forth at least two buses decked out with flags and messages announcing that this was the last day for riding on a local RT. Catford RT 2146 leaves the 'Chandos' stand at Brockley Rise on route 94, giving a handful of enthusiasts their last ride on an AEC Regent south of the river. From the following day, to ride on an RT would involve a trek over to Barking. *John Reed.*

FAREWELL

At the start of 1979, the only RTs still in revenue-earning service with LT were to be found working from Barking garage, deep in suburban east London. Their main haunt was the curiously shaped route 62, which at that time ran from Barkingside High Street via Hainault, Chadwell Heath and Upney, to Barking Gas-coigne Estate, with some Sunday journeys being extended to the picturesque Creekmouth Power Station! A narrow bridge on the route at Chadwell Heath station had spared the 7ft 6in wide RTs because LT feared the consequences of anything wider running the risk of meeting another bus halfway across the bridge. With no immediate prospect of the bridge being rebuilt, LT decided to divert route 62, which could be done without too much inconvenience to local passengers. With the last obstacle removed, it was an easy matter to find a dozen *Routemasters* and the very last RTs were finally displaced from their last duties.

Above, left: A few days before the end of the RT, 2541 pauses at the traffic lights at the bottom of East Street in Barking. It still looks smartly turned-out and a credit to its owner, despite the absence of the triangular bonnet badge, probably stolen by some eager collector. It is strange to think that at the time it was one of only 12 RTs still left in service, from a once colossal fleet of nearly 7,000 vehicles. *LT Museum 19391-8.*

Top, right: The last RT in service was No. 624, which left Barkingside on its final trip around mid-day, on Saturday April 7 1979. It was filled with enthusiasts paying their last respects, and passenger saloons were festooned with streamers and ballons. Officially speaking, for its trip from Gascoigne Estate to the garage the bus was out of service and should not have been carrying passengers, but no-one could have coaxed these people out of their seats! As the bus arrived back at Barking garage it was met by enthusiastic crowds, many of whom ventured up to the verandah of the maisonettes opposite the garage - to the apparent annoyance of the residents. With police outriders and officials in attendance RT624 was escorted effortlessly towards the garage. *LRT News.*

Above, right: Back in the garage the crew, driver John Caygill and conductor Alf White, sign autographs in a brief and bewildering moment of fame. They had brought an era to a close. *LRT News.*

REVIVAL IN THE '80s

Below: Look who's back! It's December 1986 and in brilliant blue and silver livery, RT 3232, which started life as a Green Line 'coach' at Romford garage in August 1950, pulls away from a stop in The Drive, Ilford, on Ensign route 145, won on tender from LRT earlier in the year. This was the first occasion than an RT had carried fare-paying passengers on a genuine London bus route since April 1979. *John Reed.*

Right: RT's worked in 1989, not in Fulham, Farringdon or Forest Gate, but in other places such as here at Felstead. This typical Essex village is served every Sunday in summer by route 622 (Harlow-Great Yeldham), operated for Essex County Council by Blue Triangle, of Rainham. Here, RT 2150 is passing through Felstead in June 1989. RTs may have lasted 50 years, but they are a long way behind the Church of the Holy Cross, just visible on the right, parts of which date back to the 13th century. *John Reed.*

A good number of RTs are privately preserved and may be seen at the numerous bus and coach rallies held around the country each year. The pictures on this page and overleaf are just a selection of the buses which appeared at the 1989 Southend Bus Rally. They included pre-war RT 113. Bus preservation looks set to be a pastime which will keep enthusiasts happily occupied for years to come. The RT's successors, the *Routemasters* with their non-corrosive aluminimum bodywork, are also now targets for preservationists.

Above: RT 981 and *Routemaster* RM 2198 stand side by side at the 1989 Southend Bus Rally.

Left: Blinded for Victoria, RT 1790 forms part of the display at the Southend Bus Rally, held in the RT's Jubilee year of 1989. *Both: John Reed.*

Right: Pre-war RT 113, photographed at the 1989 Southend Bus Rally. The bus is carrying adverts for *Picture Post,* a once highly-successful magazine which specialised in quality photo-journalism. Sadly, the magazine was a victim of changing tastes and the growth in importance of television, whose increasingly vivid and instant news programmes undermined its appeal. *Picture Post* disappeared from the news stands on June 1 1957.

Below: Also at the Southend Bus Rally, a trio of RTs pose for the photographer. They are (left-right): RT 3251, RT 1677 and RT 1790. *Both John Reed.*

BIBLIOGRAPHY

RT – The Story of a London Bus; Ken Blacker *(Capital Transport, 1979)*
An RT Family Album; *(Bandwagon, 1978)*
The London RT Bus; J.S. Wagstaff *(Oakwood Press, 1972)*

Periodicals:
The London Bus Magazine; *(London Omnibus Traction Society, Quarterly, various issues)*